30 Y

30 V

Barbican Theatre, Plymouth:
The People, The Place, The Art

PAMELA PETER-AGBIA

University of Plymouth Press

Paperback edition first published in the United Kingdom in 2011 by University of Plymouth Press, Roland Levinsky Building, Drake Circus, Plymouth, Devon, PL4 8AA, United Kingdom.

ISBN: 9781841022789

A CIP catalogue record of this book is available from the British Library

Editor / Contributor: Kate Campbell
Designer: William Hibberd

Printed and bound by Matrix Marketing and Media Solutions Ltd.
Unit 17, Mary Seacole Road, The Millfields, Plymouth, PL1 3JY

barbican theatre

To offer as many people as possible, but especially the young, access to, participation in, and enjoyment of high quality artistic activity, without prejudice. This is practiced in the belief that such involvement cultivates, inspires and enthuses individuals and communities to explore and express ideas and needs, voice opinions, celebrate together and agitate to provoke social and cultural change.

CONTENTS

FOREWORD

We are celebrating 30 years of the Barbican Theatre with 30 stories from people who have come through the organisation. They are symbolic of everyone who has worked with us, whoever and wherever you are. There have been thousands of young people, teachers, actors, community development workers, individuals and friends who have supported us over the years. Each one of you has made a unique contribution to the life of the theatre, sharing our vision to empower and enable as many people as possible to have access to the arts.

30 years ago, the company started with an ambition to use creativity to enhance and transform education. We have branched out since then reaching audiences and participants from all sectors of society but education and skill development is at the heart of the organisation – believing as we do that art helps people to transform their lives. Year on year our faith in the process has given us the determination to go on, using the artistic work to make the case for us.

We feel deeply privileged to work in this sector and we know the value of what we do. We hope that through reading the stories contained in this book you will recognise the value too. A huge thank you to everyone who has been with us on the journey so far.

HISTORY

The Barbican Theatre Company was set up in September 1980 as a professional outreach Theatre-in-Education organisation (called Rent-a-Role Drama Service) touring new work to schools in Plymouth, Cornwall and Devon. In 1986 the city council bought the Barbican Theatre (then Serenade Arts) as a home for the company who then paid a peppercorn rent. In 1998, the theatre was re-furbished with a capital lottery grant bringing the whole building back into public ownership.

For the past ten years the Barbican Theatre Company has evolved the role and function of the venue to respond to the needs of young people, emerging and professional artists in the city and the South West region. As a small-scale touring venue it has been a first house for companies. It has been the focus of community theatre, youth theatre and youth dance activity as a way of bringing forward new talent and potential and it has been a vital lifeline for local and regional artists as a creative space for making new work.

At the same time the Barbican Theatre Company has continued its thirty year history in socially engaged practice, specialising in making new theatre and dance in response to needs identified from communities and the statutory and voluntary sector. This has included new performance works, training, advocacy, awareness raising and conflict resolution tailored for specific audiences and participants. Previous work includes commissions from education, police, prison service, social services, drug & alcohol services, health, trade unions, probation, youth offending, BME groups and youth service.

The company were the first in the SW to argue and achieve arts funding for health and welfare initiatives from The National Lottery Charities Board. The company were the first in the city to achieve significant resources from Big Lottery Fund to use the arts as an integration tool for Black and Minority Ethnic young people and white young people in the city. Each piece of work has served as action research, evolving the organisation's understanding of contemporary issues and the role of the arts in contributing to civil and national life.

Our ability to develop new talent and potential across theatre, dance and performance arts and our ability to use the arts to engage in dialogue and debate across social issues makes us unique in our field.

BARBICAN THEATRE

FOUNDERS

The value of creative work is something that needs to be constantly explored and reasserted. It would be tempting to fall into the trap of measuring everything by its cost and nothing by its value. When this happens, something is lost which can't quite be accounted for or reclaimed. This book is written from the perspective that value comes first.

For an organisation to move forward and keep its work valuable, change is also very important. Organisations need to be able to respond to society's needs and what communities around them need. Small scale arts organisations are versatile; they are able to move, adapt and evolve with the times fairly quickly, to create work that best serves their communities and audience. What is essential, though, is a core vision, a belief and constant integrity in what you're doing.

The Barbican Theatre formed around experiments in arts education. It started with the idea that art can revolutionise the way people learn and the way people think about the world, their communities and themselves. There was the vision to make, produce, and develop high quality theatre and dance that reached out and was relevant to people's lives. The founders of The Barbican Theatre formed around this shared vision.

Rent a Role
BARBICAN THEATRE
RISK TAKING!
MARKS & SPENCER
Pay
or order
love
care
happiness

DAVID ODDIE

Founder of The Barbican Theatre and ARROW, Lecturer in Drama at University College Plymouth

My background is in teaching, so when I became an actor I wanted to work in theatre and education. I came to Plymouth in September 1980 with this idea of doing something between drama, theatre and education. That's how Rent-A-Role was born. It started in my living room as a one-man-band and I started to build up contacts with all the schools.

When the Theatre Royal was first built, I'd written a paper for the council about the Drum Theatre. It was called 'The Role of The Drum', and it was about an alternative vision for it as a community and young people's theatre. One day, Andrew Welsh, at the theatre, rang me up and said 'would you like to do what you wrote about at a theatre on the Barbican'? I did. I negotiated funding from the bank and Rent-A-Role became the Barbican Theatre. At that time the theatre was virtually a pile of rubble, there were leaks and buckets everywhere, it was a mess but we stuck at it, we had the vision.

"The Barbican is a place where you can go and do something you couldn't do anywhere else. It's also a theatre for people who wouldn't normally go to a theatre and this has always been really important."

We established a good reputation as a theatre and education company working out in the community. We were employing actors to do work in schools. The vision for the building was to create opportunities for the community to come into the theatre, so it would be a two way process. It would be organic. However, there was no money to run the theatre - there was just us. So we cobbled together a scheme for a festival. We opened up our doors and invited schools from all over the city to come and bring their work here. We had loads of people coming in, loads of stuff coming in. It ranged from the utterly crap to the sublimely brilliant. We later built up the funds to hire a centre director, someone who could direct activities and build the Barbican Theatre. His name was Mark Laville and he came in with lots of energy and passion. He fell in love with the theatre. He really made it buzz.

It's challenging to stay true to yourself and say 'this is our integrity, this is what we do'. The theatre has evolved with the people who are there. They've stuck with the battle; they won't be knocked off course by the fluctuating attitudes of external influences. Whilst I was there the theatre was about pushing boundaries artistically. The Barbican is a place where you can go and do something you couldn't do anywhere else. It's also a theatre for people who wouldn't normally go to a theatre and this has always been really important. We were saying to kids everywhere, 'this is a place you can come to', and I think that ethos has been upheld superbly. Access to people who wouldn't normally have access; that inclusiveness which was important to me has been carried on.

SHEILA SNELLGROVE

Director, Barbican Theatre

People get involved in theatre for lots of different reasons and the reason I love theatre is because of its ability to transform peoples' lives. It is a social activity. It has this ability to bring people together to create commonality; common shared experiences that become rich and productive foundations for all kinds of other things, which aren't necessarily art, but might be.

My story is an example of how you can progress in the arts to be perfectly honest. I went to the Central School of Speech and Drama and I did a Diploma in theatre and teaching, which is unheard of now. It was an incredible degree that enabled me to teach and perform. In the old days I was called an actor teacher and there were a lot of theatre and education companies who had actor teachers. I taught Theatre Arts in London in a very exceptional school – it wasn't really like being a teacher because we had our own theatre and we had our own radio station so it was amazing. It was a very seminal experience in how you can revolutionise education through art and through the processes of art.

"We're involved in what I call 'transferring the means of production', in other words passing on skills that enable other people to create their own art or enterprise."

Then I came to Plymouth because David Oddie and I were in a relationship and David chose Plymouth because there was no arts education here. From the beginning we worked together and I undertook lots of different roles from being inside a company as a performer, and a director of performance, to being involved in development of work. Now my role here has changed significantly as I am the overall responsible chief executive officer. I've gained a unique bag of skills which is useful because in the future I think artists will have to have a much bigger portfolio of skills. You won't be able to survive just saying 'I am an actor', you will need to make that meaningful in different settings. I am very proud of the fact that when people have come through here they get other jobs, they move on in their profession.

I don't think it's a very easy environment here because we work fast but there is enough support and, hopefully, enough scaffolding for people to climb. I think one of the problems in society generally is that young people don't get the opportunity to show what they can do. I think that's what we are seeking to do here. We are saying, look at all this energy, look at these young people at the peak of their creativity, their imagination, their passion and their drive. Give them room to grow.

We used to run hundreds of classes here but now we see our job as increasing the capacity for lots of other people to do that work. What we are uniquely good at is training people with the skill and ability and the confidence to go out and do creative work in many different contexts. We're involved in what I call 'transferring the means of production', in other words passing on skills that enable other people to create their own art or enterprise, because the skills in themselves produce new artists and new thinkers but they also cascade out into every area of life and can change the way whole societies function. It's profound our relationship with art.

MARK LAVILLE

Artistic Director, Barbican Theatre

I joined the Barbican Theatre as Centre Director nearly 20 years ago. I'd never run a building before I came here but I thought the auditorium here was extraordinary, and that's the main reason I took the job - to work in that space. I was also very interested in the work that the company were doing, and what they wanted to do with the building. And I really wanted to not be in London for a while. I was getting sick of the rat race, and what I call Londonitis - you live there for so long and after a while, you start to believe that London is the centre of the universe and no other place is of any value. I don't think that's true at all.

We are very strategic now about how we operate. That means the company has a slightly different identity in every 5-year-cycle. And I think that's why we've survived to this day. We look ahead. The thing that hasn't changed is our core, the relationship between theatre and dance and learning, and I don't mean learning in terms of school, I mean learning generally. Human development is the key thing at the core of the organisation. Theatre and Dance are our major vehicles, the liveness of it is really important. The thing about hanging onto making things is very important.

"human development is the key thing at the core of the organisation."

We have programmed companies like Adventures In Motion Pictures, The Kosh, Peeplelykus, The Right Size, Ridiculusmus - key theatre and dance companies that have become the fundamental web of contemporary theatre and dance in this country and abroad. I'm not saying it's exclusively because of us, but we're part of the story down here in the South West. We are part of a development web.

The Barbican Theatre is an issue-based company, that's a very unfashionable phrase now, it's a 70's phrase. It sounds worthy but we make work about stuff that is of contemporary value, that matters to people today and is relevant to our lives today. Our theatre and dance work is issue driven and we are specialists at looking at sensitive issues through the arts. We don't just use the arts as a vehicle to look at issues, we meld the relationship between theatre and dance and society. It's not art for art's sake, it's art for societies sake, that's important and that's still the core of the organisation.

Access and inclusion are key parts of our work. How do you get people, who don't yet know that the arts can be a powerful tool for them and is valid for their lives, to access it? That's always been the challenge, and we've been part of investigating that over the years.

JULES LAVILLE

Dance Animateur, Barbican Theatre

Dance is a powerful medium for young people. I'm dyslexic and as a young person I struggled at school. Dance for me became the way to communicate.

I did my first contemporary dance class here, when I was 14. It was run by John Dane, who was the director of Serenade Arts, who occupied the building before it became The Barbican Theatre. It inspired me to go and train in contemporary dance performance at London Studio Centre. I went on to further my performance, dance & education skills whilst working in Canada, Paris and London.

I'm a Plymouth girl, so I came back now and again to see my family. On one occasion, I decided to pop into the theatre and met up with Andy Higginson and Vince Manna, both dancers. We went on to form a contemporary dance theatre company called DNA (Dance Not Art). Our first piece 'La Lutte', French for 'The Wrestle', was set in a wrestling ring and was highly physical, in fact, I broke my nose and fell in love during the making of this work.

'La Lutte' toured throughout the South West and to The Place, in London. I became more involved with The Barbican Theatre and went on to develop a diverse programme of dance activity, which became a key part of what was offered by the Barbican Theatre.

'Dancers United' was one of the first projects I developed. It involved developing choreography and performance skills with teachers, community leaders and dance artists. They would then perform their choreographic work at one of the 'Dancers United' platforms, which took place across the city over a week long festival. The project enabled us to make real connections with many schools, community groups, regional dance companies artists and cultural organisations. The concept of Dancers United has evolved into 'In The Flesh', which has a very similar performance ethos.

"The Barbican Theatre is more than a building; it's not just a place where people go to dance or act."

The Barbican Theatre is more than a building; it's not just a place where people go to dance or act. We're very accessible; for many people it's like coming home, for others it's sometimes the only place they have social interaction outside of their homes. It's a creative buzzing social hub. It's not cold, administrative or corporate, it leads from the heart. I know that sounds very corny but we are passionate about what we do and how that impacts on Plymouth communities and beyond. We seek to replicate the environment of the building wherever we go. Whereever we are, we seek to cultivate the same conditions that enable as many people as possible to engage in the arts.

After graduating I found it really difficult to find my way into the industry; finding where to place myself and how to transfer my skills was a long journey. I just wish there had been more organisations like The Barbican Theatre to help. I'm happy to be part of an organisation that provides a bridge for young people into this rewarding and fulfilling industry.

JO LOYN

Head of Drama, Saltash Community College

I came to Plymouth in 1980 to work for Drumbeat. This was before the Theatre Royal had been built and we worked out of a warehouse in Cattedown. David and Sheila ran youth theatre from there. Drumbeat was to be the community theatre that worked out of the The Drum, hence the name. The idea was for us to build an audience for the main theatre through our work in schools, pubs and clubs in the city. When the Theatre Royal opened in the mid 80's there were big cuts to the arts. Drumbeat was one of the casualties. Community, participation and outreach are always the first to go. I think it's completely wrong, but there you go.

I went off to work with Red Ladder in Leeds and Dr Fosters and I said I would never come back to Plymouth because it was such a difficult city for an artist to work in. My reasons for coming back were personal, I was in a relationship with someone here, I had children, and then of course you need local work.

I worked with the company a lot as an actor in Theatre In Education programmes. I also started directing with the company and worked with the police, social services and mental health on a play called Forbidden Fire. I was an associate artist, valued as part of the company and involved in decision-making processes as a trustee.

"The Barbican Theatre puts young people first."

When the work is good and you have a whole group of young people transfixed by theatre there is nothing better, its inspirational. When it's bad, it's awful because in schools there is no hiding place. You go out without scenery – just a few props and a simple costume and you have to capture your audience purely through your acting skills and the power of the story you've come to tell. I've been in theatre programmes where young people have done extraordinary things because of the power of the experience. Children have stood up and taken on adults who they feel are behaving badly, they've found a voice and articulated the reasons why they should be better. Straight theatre never had the same pull for me; I wanted to get people thinking, believing they have the power to change things for the better.

I also set up an actor's cooperative called SWAM – South West Actors Management at the Barbican Theatre. They had space and wanted to support the idea, we got it for free. This enabled actors to look for work. It was partially successful but there were not quite enough actors to really make it effective. I worked as an actor for 20 years and I feel deeply sad about not being able to continue. When I started out there were 52 week contracts, by the time I finished there were 3 week contracts. That was the massive shift in arts subsidy.

The Barbican Theatre puts young people first. In school it helps them to think about the world and others and out of school it helps them to create their own work. This is the strongest thing about them. My son has had a connection with the theatre since he was four years old and it has made him the person he is.

Of course it's changed over the years, it has evolved. At first it was theatre out of a suitcase and now it gets people in and tells them, 'this is your building, what do you want to make? You make it and take it out.'

FIRST HOUSES

The Barbican Theatre is a 'first house' for artists and communities to try things out. First houses provide a safe space where ideas are sparked, boundaries are pushed and the hard graft is done to create excellent art. The theatre has opened its doors to many talented artists. Some of the people who have come through the building have gone on to achieve great things. Here the work of the theatre speaks for itself.

VINCE MANNA

Actor, Choreographer & Drama Teacher at London Academy of Music and Dramatic Art (L.A.M.D.A)

Theatre wasn't my culture. None of my family were theatre-goers. I probably went to see a play twice in my life before I got involved. My sister did an A-Level in Theatre Studies at Plymouth College of Further Education and I remember going to help her with a puppet show and I really enjoyed it. I was just drawn to this wonderful world where you get to be someone else. So I did the A-Level course as well. A chap on the course told me about a new youth theatre. I was a bit scared because I had very little performance experience but it just completely revolutionised my life. I got here and I thought 'who are these amazing people talking about these amazing things?' I joined and got hands on practical work led by a genius man called Mark Laville. That time was really instrumental in kick-starting a career for me. I got to learn movement, singing, text, pretty much everything at the same time. We were getting our fill of absolutely everything.

Our first performance was 'An Awkward Symphony'. It was the first time I'd performed in front of lots of people. After that I was hooked and I stayed with the theatre for many years. It became my home. I was watching the youth theatre group one day and I don't know what possessed me but I said to Mark,'can I do something with them?' I did some games and bits and pieces. Then he decided to let me run the 12-15 year-olds theatre group. We made a piece called 'Afraid Of Stepping Out' which was about confronting phobias and that's the first piece I got to direct

"That time was really instrumental in kick starting a career for me. I got to learn movement, singing, text, pretty much everything at the same time. We were getting our fill of absolutely everything."

I came to watch everything at the theatre. One of the first things I saw was Matthew Bourne's 'Adventures In Motion Pictures', this was before the 'Swan Lake' days. It was smaller scale work like 'Town & Country', 'Deadly Serious' and 'Highland Fling'. It taught me dance can be witty and fun and strongly driven by narrative. I was inspired. Mark taught me that one person can do several things and so I got this wonderfully rich education in movement, acting and directing. From there I went on to do a BTEC in Performing Arts at South Devon College in Torquay, which was 9-5 theatre every day - production, design, directing, acting, media studies. Off the back of that - at 23 - I decided to focus on dance.

All of the Dance Schools were in London so I left Plymouth and went up to London to make my fortune with £100 and a back pack! I'm happy to say I made it in dance, and I made it in theatre and now I'm lucky to be teaching and it's wonderful to give something back. It was good that the theatre came along for me. It just changed me. My feelings for the place and the people are huge. It's such an important venue, what the people are trying to do there is important and it deserves to endure.

MATTHEW BOURNE

Award winning Choreographer & Director of New Adventures

I fell in love with theatre early on and tried to get into acting, but I didn't like using my voice. Dance seemed to become an expression of something that I could speak with; telling stories without words. At 22, I did a degree in Dance Theatre at Laban. From that came the company, Adventures In Motion Pictures, which was instigated for no other reason than a group of friends wanting to work together.

I can date my life by shows - the first one we did at the Barbican was Town and Country. It was the first full length piece that I did, and that's where the company as people know it now really properly started. Town & Country was a patchwork piece made up of lots of different bits of music about Englishness. It was a little unusual and therefore it sort of won over the audience because it was unexpected. Around that time, we were National Dance Company of the South West so we came to Plymouth regularly and we built up a relationship with the theatre and slowly built up an audience around word of mouth.

One of the things I remember is turning up to the Barbican and going to the box office on the morning of a show. I'd ask 'How many people have booked?'. They'd say '35' and I'd think 'Oh, that's good'. They'd say, 'we hope to double that by tonight' and I'd say 'WOW'. I'd get very excited by that, that anyone had parted with their money to buy a ticket. It's funny to think of the difference now, but in a way it's still the same, it's still people.

I remember ironing my own costume in that little corridor backstage, helping with the scenery, there was no sitting around in the dressing room waiting to go on stage. It was busy and it was a lot of fun. It was always a very knowledgeable audience – they were enthusiastic so it was a great place to do something early on and to try things out, because it felt like the audience were with you. They vocally showed you what they felt about something. It was really useful.

"It was a great place to do something early on and to try things out, because it felt like the audience were with you."

I remember one particular show we did called 'The Percy's of Fitzrovia' - which was about the Bloomsbury Set. It had gone down so well at the Barbican, people were laughing in hysterics. We were thinking 'Wow, we've got a hit on our hands'. Then we got to The Lyric, Hammersmith and performed there - it was absolutely dire, awful reviews from all the dance critics. It was a complete shock. It just goes to show that the audience needs to trust you. With a smaller audience and venue, you're much more aware of reaction, you can feel them in the room. Often people will stick around afterwards and have a chat. You get to talk to people and it helps you with your work, it becomes a dialogue. You don't have that sort of contact with the bigger theatres; you can play to thousands of people and come out afterwards to find they've all gone home.

Liz White

LIZ WHITE

Television, Film & Theatre Actress

"Being in that dark space was really like an epiphany I remember what I was wearing the first day I was here. I remember faces that I've never seen since those years but because of something that they did in a two minute improvisation, I'll never forget."

When you want to act, people will say anything to change your mind, they'll tell you how hard it is but I always knew I wanted to do it. I joined the youth theatre at The Barbican when I was 11 or 12. It was my first experience of theatre and the time where I realised my ambitions of becoming an actress and it will always have a special place in my heart. Being in that dark space was really like an epiphany. I remember what I was wearing the first day I was here. I remember faces that I've never seen since those years but because of something that they did in a two minute improvisation, I'll never forget. It was the first place that I felt the thrill of being onstage and I knew that was what I wanted to do ultimately. I made lifelong friends in this building.

My parents were really great; they drove me here and picked me up every week because the buses were crap. I don't know if anyone else from the youth theatre went on to act professionally. I know some realised early on they didn't want to do it, or that they just wanted to do it for fun, whereas I was more annoying and precocious.

Youth theatre was free and it was for everyone - there was no audition process. It was about inclusion and recognition. It was a place where you weren't judged and compared to everyone else, it respected the spirit of youth theatre, everybody respected each other and you were celebrated for who you were. It really increased my confidence and it made me believe I was valid. School didn't give that to me. For that reason, I would really encourage any young person to go to youth theatre; you don't need to want to be an actor. The biggest things I took from youth theatre were confidence and dedication - that has filtered through into everything I've done in my career. Mark expected commitment, he expected us to turn up to rehearsals each week, and we did, if you didn't, you risked losing your place and you just didn't belong there. Determination, confidence and commitment are the biggest things I've taken with me. At that age, confidence is a big thing, and I didn't get it from anywhere else.

I worked at the National Theatre this year, I can honestly say at that age I didn't even know it existed. Places like that weren't on my radar so I didn't know the difference between being in London and being in Plymouth. It certainly didn't stop me from being an actor, why on earth would it? You know, I don't come from a theatre background, when we were here, it wasn't about what was going on elsewhere, it was very much about the here and now and what this place was doing next. So definitely, irrespective of where you come from you can find a little community group anywhere. Don't worry about your location, don't even let it bother you. Look for it on your doorstep and let your desire lead you, don't worry about anything else.

I found myself in the rehearsal watching EAST by Berkhov. Mark was directing and performing and I had an epiphany, a real theatrical experience.

CONNOR MCINTYRE

Television & Theatre Actor

The Barbican Theatre is my spiritual home and long may it continue. When I'm in the ground, I hope its doors are still open. I was selling double glazing and it was bad stuff. On one of my breaks, I walked into the theatre, and spoke to Margaret Jones. I asked what was going on, and she told me they were rehearsing a play upstairs. So I asked 'Can I go and watch?' That's how naive I was - I'd never been in a theatre.

I found myself in the rehearsal watching EAST by Berkhov. Mark was directing and performing and I had an epiphany, a real theatrical experience. How extraordinary, to turn up at a theatre and ask to watch a rehearsal and to be given access. I can't imagine another theatre in the country where that would happen. They'd call the police for you.

I was around 29, 30, quite late in the game. But, once the thought strikes you that life is short, the question is 'Why wouldn't you do it?'. It was so exciting. I don't want to romanticize things, but this is how it is. I practically hadn't read a book until I was that age and went in there. All of a sudden people are giving you scripts and plays and you go 'wow'. I was very, very lucky.

It's funny even coming into the building, what feelings I get. It's changed so much, it's got this great facility downstairs in the B-Bar now - when I was here it was a dark empty space, there were leaks everywhere and we knew where the buckets had to be. The seats were falling apart and I think the sound system was just one old speaker. As always, it was a kick and a scramble for resources and money. It was just running off the will of the people in the organisation. This was all started in David and Sheila's front room, they started Rent-a-role because they knew that kind of activity was important, to go into schools, make it fun, make it inclusive. Give people a chance to express themselves and to enrich their lives.

The door is always open, nobody is excluded. This place is about access, empowerment and giving people a place to express themselves. Whatever you go on to do in life, that experience will stand you in good stead. It's fantastic for your confidence, and for your understanding of the wider world and as an introduction to the arts. When I look at the people that have come through here, I think 'WOW'. Some have gone on to have national profiles and real success. I don't really understand dance, I don't respond to it in a strong way, but we did extraordinary weekend workshops here with Matthew Bourne - an extraordinary artist. There's Vince Manna who went on to play the male lead in Swan Lake, Liz White, who was in 'Life on Mars' and many, many others. Maybe some have gone on to be doctors or firemen but their experience will have enriched them for sure.

I'm now studying Fine Art and Art History and it's proving to be another extraordinary experience. There's a common language between the arts, which I find fascinating. It's a way that people can express themselves. Had I not had my connection with the theatre, none of these things, including my enquiry into the art world, would have ever taken place. I've just turned 50 and to still be inquisitive, to still be prepared to take a chance, to still be prepared to follow an instinct, or a serendipitous happening is great. I got that here.

PETER OSWALD

Playwright

How did I get involved with the Barbican Theatre? It was through someone called Kate Sparshatt. I met her when I was the writer-in-residence at The Globe Theatre in London. She recommended me to Mark Laville and we met to talk about his project 'Other People's Shoes'. Until that point I was aware of the Barbican but I didn't really know much about them, I had heard of them because a couple of people in my theatre company 'Hearts Tongue' had links with them.

From that meeting with Mark, I wrote a play called 'Blighty' which was about a right-wing racist youth who falls in love with a Sikh girl. She is present in his room as an imaginary person. He only actually sees her for real once at the beginning and once at the end. Part of the research for it involved me driving around Birmingham with a guy called Chas. We drove to a Gurdwara Temple where asylum seekers come and tell their stories; Romanians and Sikhs too. They come and talk about their culture.

For me it was very powerful to work directly with the source material. I had access to Chas so what I was writing was linked directly into the culture. What I learnt directly went straight into the play. There aren't many theatres where that would happen. It was extraordinary being driven around Birmingham by Chas. I saw the place through his eyes. We went to the Somali district, the Islamic district, the Sikh district. It was all these different tribes. I saw boarded up churches of previous cultures.

It is always dangerous to approach theatre with an issue-based perspective but I really did enjoy doing that. Up until that point I had written about the difference between cultures and races but not in modern times. 'Blighty' had an element of going into the psyche as well as a fairy-tale element. We had two performances at the theatre and also told the story to schools. Writing is an isolated occupation and what I did with them was a link for me to the schools. I found it interesting going in and talking to young people about racism and pre-conceptions. It was a great impetus to write something that was accessible to both adults and children.

"what they do is by the people, for the people, with the people."

I spent ten years working with The Globe Theatre and they are all about form. The Barbican is more integrated. It's about content and form together, facilitating both at once. It's extraordinary what they do in the community; it's a social centre as well as a theatre. There always seems to be this energy coming from somewhere. When I did my work with them I was suffering from The Globe. It was a joy to escape and sit in the pub with Mark and Chas surrounded by pictures of Beryl Cook!

I dipped my toe into the water with The Barbican. I would like to work with them again because what they do is by the people, for the people, with the people.

OPEN DOORS

The Barbican Theatre reaches out to communities by taking work to new and unusual settings. This makes it possible for a wider range of people to experience the arts and engage with it in different ways. For some, theatre and dance is purely a social activity and for others it's a bridge into a whole new world. Either way it allows new voices to emerge that may not have been heard before.

AZO SALM

Actor

"The Barbican theatre is the first place I went when I couldn't speak English and they were generous and supportive throughout my whole journey of being in this country. They have a good heart for the community."

I used to go to a place called Refugee First at Virginia House where I did English classes and it was a great opportunity to socialise with other refugees. One day I was talking with someone, I told them I was an actor and this woman asked me if I wanted to do some acting over here. Of course I said yes, and she took me to The Barbican Theatre. They were in the middle of rehearsing for their pantomime, Puss In Boots.

The first person I met was Sheila Snellgrove. It was a strange meeting because the person I was with said 'this is Azo' and Sheila pretended to faint because the week before they had been working with an Iraqi called Azo, he had just left and then in I walked, another Azo from Iraq! They ended up giving me the main part for Puss In Boots – I couldn't believe it, my English wasn't good and I was given the part of Pip. It took me three months to learn. The theatre put the script on tape for me and I used a walkman to learn it. I used to walk around the theatre learning the words.

I was offered a paid acting job with them at the end of 2003, working on 'Arabian Nights', by then my English had improved a lot. Over time I built up a friendship with the theatre - I've been working with them now for nine years and have a very good relationship with them. Last year in particular, I worked on a project that was taken into schools called 'One Extreme'. It was about challenging racism. For me, they were the right people to do this. I trusted them to deliver on such an issue – about something that has affected me and many other people on a daily basis.

The Barbican Theatre is the first place I went when I couldn't speak English and they were generous and supportive throughout my whole journey of being in this country. They have a good heart for the community. They're very important to me.

I was working on Arabian Nights with 100 people, of all ages, but I was the only non-white face. I was the only person being paid – I was the only professional. Rod Dixon, the director at the time, introduced me. He said 'this is Azo and he is a professional actor'. It was like I was Brad Pitt! We had a party in the bar, after we'd finished the play and when I went everyone said goodbye and gave me a hug. It was a great moment. I was introduced to these people from the outside world and I wasn't an alien. I was a refugee, not a monster. The costume designer stood up in front of everyone and said thank you to me for changing her perspective. 'I used to think differently about refugees' she said and she did that in front of all those other people. When I found them it felt like I was home.

Luke Thorne

LUKE THORNE

Performer with Strictly Collaborative

"I wanted people to realise that just because I've got a disability it doesn't mean I can't do anything. So I'm doing as much as I can in my power to make people have different thoughts about me."

The way I see things everyone's disabled, no-ones perfect. Some people's disabilities are on the inside, and they may not get discriminated against because people don't see it. People only discriminate against people who have a disability that's easily noticeable. I've been discriminated against for most of my life.

I did my Bronze Arts Award through the National Children's Home with a woman called Rachel Clarke. I made two films, one called 'Discrimination Prohibited', another called 'Relevant Lives'. 'Relevant Lives' was a short film about a blind social care worker. 'Relevant Lives' was about getting people with disabilities to have pride and confidence in themselves, to go out and do things, and to have relevant lives. I acted in both of them. After I did the bronze, I didn't want to stop. I wanted to move forward and get the silver and the gold. That's how I got involved with the Barbican Theatre. I did my silver award with Dienka Hines, through Collective Voices. She was great company and really easy to work with.

For my silver award I did lots of different things. I produced my own radio show exploring discrimination in more depth, with this show, I wanted to get more people out there to think about what causes discrimination, how it feels to be discriminated against and how it can be stopped. I interviewed different people in the community about their views on disability. These included the head teacher of a special school for disabled children, a disabled practitioner setting up her own theatre company and a mental health support worker. The show was broadcast on the Freesound FM community radio station.

I am doing my gold now and have made a film called 'Are You Listening?!'. Its about young people in the care system telling their stories. I worked with a professional film maker, Fiona Evans. I have also been working with Strictly Collaborative, a disabled-led theatre company for 13-25 year olds. I wanted to get involved with them because I wanted people to realise that just because I've got a disability it doesn't mean I can't do anything. So I'm doing as much as I can in my power to make people have different thoughts about me. Disability isn't the first thing people should see in me. There are a lot of people with disabilities that can actually do a lot for themselves.

When I finish doing my Arts Award, I'm not going to give up. I'm going to carry on doing things. I've enjoyed theatre ever since I started here, I've always liked acting, I've always liked being on film. I'm a get up and go type of person. Doing these things makes me feel proud of myself.

ADRIAN ANDRASZ

Breakdancer

I came over here from Poland about ten years ago with my whole family. I used to fight on the streets in gangs for money there. From the age of 9 or 10 I was fighting so that I could get money to buy food. You used to get £10-£15 per fight and that was a lot. It was hard to survive. If you had no money you survived on water and climbed trees to get fruit to eat. To explain the money to my mother, I told her I was helping old people – it was only about a year ago that I told her I had actually been fighting.

I was out looking for my brother one day on the streets in Poland and I saw him doing some street dancing. I came down to have a closer look and was pushed into the circle and that was it. I was a natural – better than all of them! Then I came over here and began dancing with a group called the Beat Breakers with my brother.

"I'll never forget the first time I came in, I was made so welcome. Someone gave me a big hug and said hello."

We were asked to come and perform at the theatre as part of the Respect Festival. Then we needed somewhere to teach and we started break dance and street dance classes and it got really busy and we worked out a friendship with the theatre. Eventually we organised a break dance competition here. All of us who were involved in the street dance community realised that this place was really good. They also asked me if I wanted to become part of their Day of Difference programme, where you go into schools and get a chance to make a change, tell them what is really happening to people of different backgrounds and race. The teachers always say that some of them are going to play up but as soon as people hear our voices and our stories it hits them really hard and you see an instant change in their faces.

The people at the Barbican are really nice, the doors are always open. For me, it's one of the best places in Plymouth for artists, for anyone who wants to try things out. It's free. You can be yourself, no-one's judging you. It's such an accessible place. Now I'm a self-employed street dance and acrobatic teacher and I wouldn't have got there without the theatre.

I'll never forget the first time I came into the building, I was made so welcome. Someone gave me a big hug and said hello. Afterwards I went home and told my mum. I told her to go down to the theatre and have a look for herself, because she doesn't go out much. She sometimes goes into town but she doesn't enjoy the experience. When she came here she said it was lovely.

The Barbican is important for people out there who don't have opportunities. It opens doors for anyone, it gives them opportunities in life and gives them confidence in themselves. This place changed many things for me – it gave me the knowledge and the confidence to take my dancing to the next level. Coming here I felt like I was learning something every day. I always took something home with me.

KELLY MCGRATH

City College Plymouth Student

I came here in September 2009. My young carers' worker told me about a project called 'Voices For Change'. So I came down and I've stayed ever since. The first thing we got to work on was ARROW. ARROW stands for Arts - A Resource for Reconciliation all Over the World. It's about young people getting together to create change using the arts. We did student leadership workshops and got to lead our own at the ARROW congress. We fundraised for a group of young people from India to attend. We did bag-packing at Sainsbury's and wrote to the Youth Opportunity Fund to get funding for our accommodation.

There were about 100 of us from all over the world at the congress. We created small theatre pieces in groups and then we did a piece together and took it out to the streets. Our play was about a grey Plymouth and a colourful Plymouth. The grey people didn't want the colourful people coming in because they were different so they set up a wall. But some of the grey people and some of the coloured people became friends anyway. It was about not wanting change to happen. It was really good to be a part of it. I met people from all over the world and I'm still in contact with them now. It was an amazing week, the best week of my life. It changed my perception of many things and I learnt so much about how different people's lives were. People from countries I'd never even heard of were there. At the end of the week we all brought something that was personal to us and did a swap. I got a hand-made cup from Sierra Leone.

"I met people from all over the world and I'm still in contact with them now. It was an amazing week, the best week of my life."

At Voices For Change we make plays and do workshops. At the moment I'm making a short film to raise awareness about young carers. I'm going to put the film onto DVD and send them out to schools. I didn't know I was a young carer until I was 11. You don't know you are one when you've lived it all your life. I want people to know I'm no different to anyone else, I just have more responsibilities. I'm still a kid and I still want to have fun. I look after my brother, and when he was younger if I wanted to do anything or go anywhere I'd take him with me. That's how he got involved with Voices for Change because no-one could look after him one day. So he came here with me and he's stayed ever since. It's the only group that he's stayed in and hasn't been kicked out of which is great.

I've met some really nice people through 'Voices for Change'. Even the ones that have left, I'm still in touch with. We have been given loads of opportunities to do things. I went to France with Alix Harris for a play called 'House On The Border' last year. That was my first time abroad. I never cared about French at school, because I never thought I'd have to use it, but I felt really rude not knowing their language. I love that no matter where you're from, the Barbican Theatre is always open.

CLARE WATERFIELD

Dance Teacher

"When we dance together we're all like little kids, we run around and squeal with laughter until tears stream down our faces. It's about having a safe environment where you can let go and be yourself."

Dance is very good if you're shy, which I am. My parents sent me to classes because they thought it would do me good. I didn't speak to my dance teacher for 3 years! Remarkably, at the age of 14 or 15 I was teaching dance to my peers. When you're in that space it's like acting, you become someone else, you relax.

At 20 I gave up dancing to take up a career in nursing. Twelve years later, in 1996, I discovered the theatre by accident. I picked up a leaflet for dance classes. I joined because I'd just moved here and didn't know anybody. It was through those classes that I got to know people and reawakened my passion for dance. After a while I was encouraged to join in with the 'Time to Dance' project. The project was a 2-year-programme set up to go into the community and work with older people using dance. Jules Laville set up a class at the theatre first and then expanded it to a group of teachers going out into community centres and residential homes all over Plymouth.

It was a great project but it wasn't just the dance that was important, it was the social aspect as well. When the project came to an end, I said 'Do you want me to continue?' Having spent two years teaching, there was no way I could just say 'Bye, I'm not doing it anymore'. I had to carry on, I really wanted to. So I started doing my own dance classes. It enabled me to turn my hobby into a job. The Barbican Theatre is that special place in Plymouth. Most of my close friendships have all emanated from my time there. I suppose we all have that common thread - a passion for dance and theatre.

Dance has always been in me. When I stopped, I missed it. The theatre reawakened that passion. I've been able to perform, teach children and have them teach and perform with older people. It just opened up this new world for me. I was brought up in a dance school environment, so being introduced to community dance, taking dance to all sorts of people that may not have done it before was really nice. It's been a privilege. I don't see the age difference - these are young minds in old people's bodies. If you treat someone how you would like to be treated it makes a difference. When we dance together we're all like little kids, we run around and squeal with laughter until tears stream down our faces. It's about having a safe environment where you can let go and be yourself.

CULTURAL CHOICES

Plymouth has changed significantly over the last couple of decades from a predominantly white population to a multi-cultural city, where over 78 languages are spoken. New people have arrived bringing a diverse range of new cultural assets and experience with them. The Barbican Theatre is at the forefront of arts initiatives supporting community cohesion, celebrating diversity, and challenging discrimination and racism.

"I was only meant to be there for 3 months but stayed
for 4 years. I was just really interested in the work they
were doing; I was surprised by all the people I met who
were doing really progressive stuff."

DIENKA HINES

Culture Education Manager, Culture Swindon

After graduating, I found out about this thing called 'Fast Track', a programme the Independent Theatre Council were running to train Black, Asian and Minority Ethnic people as senior managers within the Arts. They sent me a list of placements to look at. The Barbican Theatre was one of them and I remember putting them straight in the 'NO' pile. I was like 'Where's Plymouth?' My Mum was offended because she was born just outside Plymouth, so I fished it back out, found out where Plymouth was and had a look at it. I went there and got a job.

I was only meant to be there for 3 months but stayed for 4 years. I was just really interested in the work they were doing; young people's work, cultural awareness work and community cohesion work. I was surprised by all the people I met who were doing really progressive stuff. More than you would think for a place like Plymouth.

I eventually ran a project called Collective Voices. It was so up my street, I could have written it myself. It was such a good opportunity. The project was about bringing young white and black people together, and getting them to do arts activities together to learn about other people's cultures. It was also a follow up project from all the social inclusion work the theatre had done. They did a programme called 'Kicking Arts', another called 'Access All Areas' - it was all about getting hard-to-reach young people who wouldn't normally get involved in the arts to do an arts programme and gain accreditation. For 'Kicking Arts', Sheila actually wrote an accreditation and got it put through the Open College Network.

We got 60 people through their Arts Awards. A lot of the young people stayed and got involved with things in the theatre. Like Luke (Thorne) - he's extraordinary. He came from the NCH (National ChildrensHome's,Care Leavers Group. I used to go and visit the group and do their arts awards with them and encourage their support workers to bring them to the theatre. It took a year to get the young people to come in on their own. I remember Luke came with his brother to see something and then he came and did Collective Voices, then work experience, then he did his silver arts award, he made an anti-discrimination dvd with the EBC, and now he's doing his gold arts award with Sheila, leading his own project. For him there's been a real journey and transformation.

Through 'Collective Voices', I got to work with so many amazing young people. I got to do so many amazing things. We did stuff for Black History Month and International Women's Day. We got performance poet Benjamin Zephaniah to perform at 'How To Change The World In 7 Days'. Again, that was all about issues people wanted to change with an anti-racism focus. By the time I came to leave, I wasn't worried about the young people because they were all off doing their own things by then.

It was such a good opportunity and the beginning of my professional career. What is special about the theatre is that people go there and grow. They don't just do projects - they grow people.

BECCA ADSHEAD

People & Families Officer, Racial Equality Council Plymouth

I came to a think tank at the Barbican Theatre during my last year of University in 2004. They had taken on a three year project aimed at raising cultural awareness, which is what I did my dissertation on. From that, a play called 'Other People's Shoes' was produced, which was taken into schools. The play was about a Sikh guy, a white racist and an Asian girl.

Culturally, Plymouth has changed rapidly in the last 10 years but there's still a huge white majority and an almost backward attitude towards racism, culture and difference in some areas. We got to the realisation that education - through theatre and drama - would be the best way to address the issues in a safe way, without wagging fingers and getting people's backs up.

I grew up in Gloucestershire. It was very much like this area and I was on the brunt of racism quite severely at school and it did shape my childhood. When I went to University and started studying, the where's and why's and history of racism, I got a real passion for it. I tried to turn all of the crap stuff into something positive that makes a difference to young people now. The work we did made a difference, we made them think, it was at least a discussion point. We talked about the issues and how it made them feel.

From that project we then developed 'Day of Difference', a day-long programme that goes into schools. At the beginning of the day, they show 10 different faces and the kids just have to write down everything that comes into their heads about all these faces - and they're all very different faces. Then they go into a role-play, refugee situation exercise. Then in the afternoon, we go in as visitors and sit around together and talk to them and they write again about their assumptions about us. Many of these children haven't come into personal contact with people from other races or cultures.

"They're forward-thinking compared to a lot of places and other organisations; you don't have to explain the issues because they've worked very hard at trying to understand the issues."

I love working with the Barbican Theatre because they hold the same values as I do. You're starting from the same page which is really important. Through Day of Difference, we have created a 'Diversity Champions' initiative. The Barbican Theatre aren't afraid to address the issues. We're doing a similar project called 'One Extreme' now, which is very powerful. We're keeping the debate open, letting young people say what they think. If they're not allowed to say what they think, you can't address it. Racism is a minefield. People are so scared to talk about it, so they don't, and it just gets pushed to the background and becomes this big white elephant, ironically.

The theatre is very proactive about being inclusive, they go out of their way to include people. They're forward-thinking compared to a lot of places and other organisations; you don't have to explain the issues because they've worked very hard at trying to understand the issues. Dealing with these things can be uncomfortable and difficult but I feel safe and supported here.

NATASHA KOSHTI

University of Plymouth Student & Dance Teacher

I live with my grandparents. My grandfather is Indian but I grew up in Plymouth. As a British Asian girl living here, I've had personal experience of racism and ignorance, which I feel have been the result of a misunderstanding of other cultures. This is made worse when there is no platform to learn about other people's backgrounds. The Mela was definitely a place for people to learn about other cultures in a fun and non-threatening way. Dance is something that everyone can relate to, so it was a good way to deliver the message that the Mela was trying to communicate.

I got involved with the Barbican Theatre through my grandfather and my father who were organising the Mela as part of the South Asian Society. I was invited to attend programming meetings, to offer a young persons' perspective on what kind of things the Plymouth Mela should entail. From those meetings I got more and more involved in the planning of the Mela and also contributed as a dancer and choreographer.

> *"It was a real fusion of contemporary and traditional influences."*

I've always danced, I learnt ballet, modern, classical and tap when I was growing up. Bollywood Dance was a fairly recent progression. In 2008 I went to India to visit my relatives and that's where I first started to take an interest in Indian dance. My grandfather's sister, my great aunt, taught me a very traditional Indian dance called Bharata Natyam and I started to do it to more modern music. When I got back, I decided to apply what I'd learnt and teach it on to other people. From there I took over a Bollywood Dance group at the University of Plymouth. I now have 25 to 30 students who I teach. I'm also contracted out to schools as part of cultural education lessons.

For the Mela, I was given the opportunity to work with professional artists, I was also involved in choreographing and performing a three minute Bollywood Dance piece called 'Bollywood Explosion'. I worked alongside Jules Laville and Vinitha Rajkumar from Rhythm India School of Dance. It was a real fusion of contemporary and traditional influences. I taught the three minute piece to dance schools across the city which ended in a public mass dance bringing both the City Centre Piazza and Drake Circus shopping centre to a stand-still on the day.

I also worked with a graphic designer from the College of Art, who was commissioned to design the Mela logo and other marketing materials by The Barbican Theatre. He created this really cool multi-media piece of me performing, which was shown on the BBC Big Screen and BBC Devon website in the lead up to the event.

I loved doing the Mela, I learnt so much. I really enjoyed it, although, as it was the first one I'm wasn't sure what to expect. Organising something of that scale was a great challenge. There was a great partnership between the South Asian Society and the theatre, and it did so much for Plymouth. I developed skills as an artist, a teacher, and also as an arts leader. The work the theatre does, organising events like the Mela, is so important. Working with them has shown me what I can do.

MATTHEW ROBINSON

Scottish Dance Theatre Company Member

I was at PYDC until I was 18 and I feel like I lived through the time of it getting really big and strong. The last thing I did was Bugs and it felt huge. We had a set and costumes, we worked with scientists and did a mini-tour. It felt so exciting. The Barbican has been a massive part of my life as a dancer and as a person. I met people there I would never have met otherwise. Usually in the dance world you meet similar people from a similar background. At PYDC there was a real cross section of people. Jules didn't take dancers on what they offered in the immediate moment but on the potential within them. The room was filled with this exciting diversity.

When I left, I moved to London to train in dance at The Place. I did a BA in Contemporary Dance. I auditioned for Laban and The Northern School of Contemporary Dance and got offered places there as well. Then I became an apprentice for the Scottish Dance Theatre based in Dundee. So far I have worked with choreographers from all over the world including Hofesh Shechter, Liv Lorent, Ben Duke, Kate Weare & Ben Levy. One of the things I feel connects me to what I am doing now is the work I did with the Barbican. I am working in a dance company with humanity and human experience at its heart and that's what it's like at The Barbican.

"As a young male dancer in a predominantly female world it was hard when I was younger."

When I moved to London I went through a weird patch where for me, it became all about my body, about sorting out my physicality. It was all about getting my ballet up to speed and I left some of what I had learnt at PYDC behind. Once I got past that, the knowledge and experience of what I had learnt came back to me because once you get beyond what your body can physically do, it's about allowing yourself to be yourself and I now carry that with me. When I was there with PYDC I never considered the impact of what I was doing. It is only now that I do. We were making real, proper art. It wasn't just about making something that looked pretty, it was about making something that mattered. I never felt it was just about getting us to dance, it was never a community experiment. It was about making the best we could, which is extremely rare in a theatre of the Barbican's type. They make groundbreaking work not just for the sake of participation but because of it.

As a young male dancer in a predominantly female world it was hard when I was younger. School was hard. I wouldn't polish over the cracks, there was bullying but I think anyone with an artistic sensibility goes through some form of bullying, but the theatre made me feel special. There we celebrated difference, so to be honest, I never worried about it. I am proud that part of my history lies with the Barbican. I feel like I have left my footprint there, that I have made my mark. That they gave me something and I gave something back.

"They truly want to include people"

RUTH MITCHELL

Co-founder of Part-Exchange Company
& Barbican Theatre Trustee

I came to Plymouth in 1999, because my partner got a job at the Theatre Royal. One of the first people I became friends with was Jack Mellor, who was a trustee of the Barbican Theatre. He told me they were looking for theatre people to sit on the board. So I came in and spoke to Sheila and the chair at the time, Robin Tatem, and I became a trustee. I'd come from London with a good theatre CV so I had a good knowledge of what other theatres were doing to bring to the table.

At the time, there were only a handful of professional actors in Plymouth. I think everybody else just left and didn't come back. It was very difficult to get work down here, I got some small parts doing local television work but generally everything else I did was in London.Travelling that distance was a real chore, it was so hard to get back home on weekends. It got to a point where I wanted to do work in the city I was living in. I also met Rachel Aspinwall around this time, who was in the same position. Together we decided to try and make work for ourselves and that's how Part Exchange Company was formed.

There's a misconception that the only cultural option in Plymouth is the Theatre Royal. It's this huge mammoth building which employs an enormous number of people but there are lots of little things going on all the time. I think the Barbican Theatre is a hub for those small things that are going on. It opens its doors to that kind of activity, when many don't. I suppose that has a lot to do with the building. To have a space of that size is very unique for a small-scale theatre house. Most theatres like The Barbican have tiny little box offices. The Barbican Theatre have a building.

When we started there was a real lack of understanding from people about what we were trying to do. And you'll still find that in Plymouth unfortunately, from people who don't like change. Other cities seem more upbeat about culture and there's a buzz. Whilst things have improved, I think Plymouth falls behind when it comes to celebrating the city. People need to be more courageous. A cities culture is what makes it vibrant, it's what brings people in.

The Theatre have always supported us. This year, we are working with Plymouth Youth Dance Company, for our next Hidden City event, 'Drive-in Deco'. So there's that partnership there also. What I love about the Theatre - and they were always the first to do this - is their commitment to bringing hard to reach people into the theatre. You can see other companies doing that now but the Barbican were doing it when no-one else was. They truly want to include people. And it's always great to see the people who come into the building and have their eyes are opened to their own possibilities.

FUTURE ARTISTS

Future Artists

New and emerging artists are the future of culture in Great Britain. The Barbican Theatre supports the next generation of makers to develop and capitalize on their artistic talent by offering space, professional experience and access to industry networks. We create new arts leaders through our Graduate Internship Programe & training companies

GINA SHERMAN

South West Regional Co-ordinator, Apples & Snakes

After Uni you have that year where it's like 'What the HELL?!'. I'd been in this wonderful bubble of creativity, at Dartington, studying Writing & Visual Arts and now the bubble had burst and I couldn't find my feet. I didn't know what to do. I eventually found a volunteer post here at the box office every Tuesday - just answering the phone and doing basic admin tasks. Then I started doing a few evenings, ushering. I got to see shows and realised that there is creative stuff going on in Plymouth.

"After Uni you have that year where it's like 'What the HELL?!'."

Slowly over time, I discovered my love for performance again. I did a piece at In The Flesh. It was terrible. We just tried to do something that we'd never done before - using bits of text and projections and going up to random objects and talking about memories. They give you that opportunity to experiment here, and although we didn't do anything like that again, I'm glad we tried it because even though it didn't work, we realised it was fun working together. It started off a partnership, and we now do cabaret, burlesque and comedy stuff.

I think the people here are brilliant. There's a lot of creativity. You have to be a little bit pushy, you have to not be afraid to speak your mind and go up and talk to people, take opportunities and grab people when you see them. But you learn that, and that's what it's like in the real world, if you just sit back and wait for people to come to you, you're not going to get very far. I think being here teaches you that.

From the box office, I got a Volunteer Co-Ordinator job at the theatre, and a Project Co-Ordinator job for Dance In Devon. I got those jobs through the experience I'd built up here. It was my first paid job in the arts, which I'd never had before.

I found out about a job opening at Apple and Snakes, I'd seen their Forked events at The B bar. I knew Mel, who was doing the job before me, and I knew the nights were great. I knew what they were about. I didn't think I was going to get it, I wasn't sure I was good enough. But when I stopped to think about it, I realised that between Dartington, Dance In Devon, and the Barbican Theatre, I did actually have good experience and good contacts.

ALIX HARRIS

Graduate Theatre Intern,

Co-founder of Promnesia Dance Theatre Company

I nearly never went to my first audition for Strange Youngens. I didn't think I was good enough and I didn't know how to get to the Barbican from where I lived. I remember driving down the dual carriage way into Plymouth thinking, 'this is ridiculous'. It was pouring with rain and I couldn't find a parking space. I turned up to my audition soaking wet and late. We had to work in pairs doing floor sequences, and text stuff, which was daunting because I hadn't done anything like that before. For one exercise, we had to stand on the spot and shout 'AAAAAAAAAAHHHHHH'. I had a throat infection but I refused to have anything else ruin my audition so I aaahhhed my way into the company.

"To be in an environment where people genuinely love theatre and have a real passion for it was precious to me."

We soon started rehearsing for One Small Step One Giant Leap, which was a promenade piece about environmentalism and human impact on the planet. The props, set and costumes were all recycled. Mark let me join the production team as a researcher. Uni had broken up for summer so I came in almost everyday. I started off as a volunteer but in the end I got paid. Our job was to research and resource everything needed for the production. We were treated like professionals and they put aside the fact that we hadn't done it before which was a real compliment. We got to sit in production meetings and worked with Mark and Nat Tarrab - the set designer - to source old mobile phones, briefcases and business suits. We collected over 2000 books from Oxfam. It was a great piece. I continued to work at the Theatre while I was at University and went on to gain experience in marketing, project management and fundraising.

I gradually got more responsibilities with Strange Youngens and started leading the young peoples group Voices for Change. At the end of my 3rd year, people started saying to me 'Alix, I wish I'd done what you did'. People on my course were asking me to look at their work, or give advice on how to start a theatre company. It was really peculiar and I thought, 'I do know this stuff, but why don't you?' That made me realise just how much I'd learnt from the theatre. I've never felt like I belonged somewhere as much as I do at the Theatre. To be in an environment where people genuinely love theatre and have a real passion for it was precious to me. I quickly got addicted to being there, I was so hungry for it - I still am.

Now I'm a graduate theatre intern and I've been able to work more closely with everyone at the Barbican. The people that work here are human, you get warmth from them. They greet you on busy days. There's laughter on crap days. There's a togetherness. They're interested in people and their journeys. You can come in with no arts experience at all, and walk out with 10 years experience after a year. They're just very loving and giving and selfless. I could pick out every brilliant word in the dictionary to describe this place, but I think you just have to experience it. It's infectious, and as soon as you enter the building, you're infected.

KERRI JACKSON

Graduate Dance Intern, Co-founder of Promnesia Dance Theatre Company

My friend went to audition for PYDC and I joined her, because she wouldn't audition on her own. I wasn't there as a dancer, or a performer, I didn't even know what popular dance was. I felt so out of place and rubbish compared to everyone else. But I joined in, and got in.

PYDC was immediately an escape from everything. I had only just turned 16 and I wasn't at home with my parents. I was working two jobs, I was living with someone, school was uninspiring, there was nothing that interested me. I wasn't thinking of continuing my education, I was literally looking at a life of working in a shop. Getting into PYDC made me realise that life hadn't been good enough. Soon I decided to do my A-Levels, so I could go to Uni because I decided pretty much half way through the first year that dance was my career. It's the only thing I really enjoyed.

The first thing I did at the theatre was the 'Bugs' project. All of the material that we generated was relevant to the theme. I was a buzzy bee and I dressed in a bee costume! I had to find out and research about the queen bee and then we went to the university and actually learnt about it properly.

Dance is so broad, you don't realise until you're doing it properly just how many different career options there are. In my 2nd year of University, I was leaning towards choreography. I had to do a placement year and my lecturer suggested I get back in touch with people that I'd feel comfortable working with, and straight away I thought of Jules. She let me assist the choreography for 'One Small Step, One Giant Leap'. I wasn't as forward and confident as I am now, but that was quite a development for me choreographically. Doing that piece, and seeing how Jules had the eye for the whole project made me think 'that's definitely what I want to do'. So for the rest of my 2nd and 3rd year, I focused on choreography.

"I wasn't thinking of continuing my education, I was literally looking at a life of working in a shop. Getting into PYDC made me realise that life hadn't been good enough."

I spent the whole summer learning about choreography and put everything I'd learned into my university work. I graduated in 2009, and won an InMotion Award for innovative performance and choreography. That was massive - I found that more important than my actual degree. And from there I got an offer to go to South Africa, to re-work that choreography for people out there. I worked with two companies, experimenting in harness work and contemporary dance. I danced on top of Table Mountain; that experience continues to inspire me as a developing choreographer. Before South Africa, I was working and volunteering at the theatre with PYDC. When I returned, I didn't actually think I was going to stay in Plymouth, because I didn't think there would be any job opportunities. But then the Plymouth Graduate Internship programme came up at the theatre.

As Dance intern, Jules has given me more responsibility when it comes to the training companies. I help co-ordinate PYDC and Strange Youngens and helped choreograph 'Alice Through The Looking Glass' - last years Christmas show. I also project manage 'In The Flesh', and have set up a dance theatre company with another intern, Alix Harris, and we're making our own work.

TOM KINDELL (KIN)

Graduate Dance & Media Intern, Choreographer

At school I was always in trouble, always fidgeting, always full of energy. I needed to run around a room and let off steam. I found this place in Nottingham where I lived, a dance and theatre place, and it was the best thing for me.

I finished my degree in 2010 at Dartington College of Art in Choreography and Visual Art, then I went to Amsterdam to do some improvising work. I came back from Amsterdam and didn't really know what to do with myself. I remembered going to watch the 'In The Flesh' festival at the Barbican Theatre, so I got in contact to see if they had any opportunities available and from there I applied for the Graduate Intern scheme.

"I've been able to work things out for myself, and through that my confidence has grown."

My role as Dance & Media intern involves loads of different things. Most recently, I've been working with Plymouth Youth Dance Company, teaching technique in dance. At Christmas I worked on the choreography and assisted on the technical stuff and multi-media stuff for 'Alice Through The Looking Glass'. I also work with 'Voices For Change', the young people's group, which is a place for anyone to come and be creative, to express themselves and to talk about issues relevant to their lives. The reward is seeing people be creative, being themselves and developing themselves.

When I was younger I was in a metal band but I was going to ballet classes in secret as well. I was living in two conflicting worlds. When the band found out they chucked me out. It was one of many negative experiences I had as a young man who loved to dance. Some of it violent - I've been beaten up five or six times, I've got fake teeth, and scars from being kicked in. Eventually I gave up, I gave up dance for a year but I became angry and fidgety again. One of the reasons I chose Dartington - I was offered places at Laban and Northern Dance - was to get away from all of that, to come down south.

Here you learn the stuff they don't teach you at school, you're totally put in the deep end. It's a sink or swim situation, which is what real life is like I guess. You have to learn to swim. I've been learning off everyone. I love that. The Barbican Theatre has definitely kick-started things for me. I feel safe and accepted here. There's an acceptance of who you are and although I've felt lost at times, I've been able to work things out for myself, and through that my confidence has grown.

"Getting into the company really built my confidence. Lack of confidence can be a really big barrier in dance, so coming here and having that opportunity helped me a lot, it proved to me that actually, I was good enough."

GEMMA WARD

Freelance Dance Teacher & Photographer

My friend dragged me along to this open DJ deck night which was being run at B-bar, I was 16 or 17. The event was being run by a youth arts group called B=MC2. Whilst there, Kate Reid, who was running the group at the time, sort of jumped on us and was like "Oooh come to the group!", so the next week we came to a meeting.

We went to B=MC2 every week - sitting around the B-bar eating curly fries after meetings became a bit of a ritual. We planned events, crew shows and more open deck nights. We also helped market events for the theatre. Soon after, I joined 'Weird Cabaret', which was run by Mark Laville. At the time it was known as Orange Wednesdays - it was sponsored by Orange - and we did a series of weekly workshops which culminated in a performance in the B-Bar, doing walk-about-theatre stuff. That then led me to the 'Dance It' classes as I was interested in dance too. The theatre's dance company PYDC was also going by then but I didn't have the guts to audition. I really admired them but I didn't think I was good enough, so I stuck to the other classes. There were always lots of things happening everywhere which I loved and everything was open and accessible.

Eventually, I did audition for PYDC but reluctantly because I get nervous and I still didn't think I was good enough. We did a class and then an improvisation. They just played the music and you had to do something, move there and then for a certain amount of time. That was my biggest nightmare, it was just like "ARGGHH!". I remember it really vividly because a lot of the girls I went to ballet class with had auditioned as well and they'd been with the company for some time. They all got calls before me because for some reason the contact number on my application form was wrong and I thought that I hadn't got in. I thought everyone else had got in apart from me. Then I got the message from Jules. I was so happy, I was literally running up and down screaming "Woooooooh!".

Getting into the company really built my confidence. Lack of confidence can be a really big barrier in dance, so coming here and having that opportunity helped me a lot, it proved to me that actually, I was good enough. In my first year, we did 'Syncapoda' which was about bugs and insects. We worked with an entomologist from The University of Plymouth to study how bugs moved and we were trained to stilt walk. I was a dragonfly so I was on big stilts with these huge wings. It was crazy, unlike anything I'd ever done before and that's what has kept me coming back. I'm too old now but I'm still in the company; I perform and support the practitioners now which are really nice.

What's really exciting for me is to see other people grow. Some of the members start with that same lack of faith in their abilities that I did when I was their age. To see them come through here and go off and do brilliant things is amazing. So many people have come through here and gone on to do great things. That's because The Barbican theatre has so much to offer. The journey and the change in me and my confidence are the best things I have got from here. I have the confidence now to perform, to facilitate things, to teach others. In my working life too. I go into schools and teach whole classes now. I would never have imagined doing that.

FLOURISH

All things start as an experiment. The opportunity to try out new ideas and show them to an audience is essential to the process of developing new work. The Barbican Theatre provides professional support to new and emerging companies to help them to flourish. This goes from in-kind support and mentoring through to co-productions that tour regionally and nationally.

YAMAHA

DIESEL
ONLY THE BRAVE

KEVIN JOHNSON

Artistic Director of Symbiotic Dance Company & Lecturer

I moved down here in 2006, from London, where I trained as an actor and a director. It was for love reasons mainly, nothing to do with work and I remember thinking this could be wrecking my career but actually it blossomed. My career didn't end here, far from it, it began. When I first got here I thought 'OK, go to a theatre'. The first person I met was Sheila. They were doing the Bugs project at the time and she had loads of mail outs to do so she chatted to me while I stuffed some envelopes for her! She said I should meet Mark so I met him, in a pub, and it went from there. Quite quickly he said "do you want to manage a festival?"

I almost fell off my chair when he asked me because it was a bold move. I had never managed a festival before, I wasn't sure I was qualified to do it but he seemed confident and said he would support and mentor me through it. Within a month I was managing the first 'In the Flesh' festival. It was phenomenal, especially coming from London where you're forever trying to batter down doors and find a way in. Big organisations have many hoops and processes and paperwork that you have to go through and lots of people saying no you aren't quite ready for that yet. The Barbican aren't like that.

"My career didn't end here, far from it, it began."

'In The Flesh' was about a diverse range of people experimenting with their art forms or with people or with concepts, to scratch out ideas and have it shown to a public audience alongside other artists. We set ourselves four different criteria; to have a range of art forms, to have collaborative practice, to get new companies seen onstage and also to get people working and networking together. We wanted to make Plymouth aware that there is a rich bed of talented artists. I think the Barbican has succeeded in becoming a centre for those people to come to. I really enjoyed it.

It was pretty stressful for that week. I was living and breathing the Barbican and the festival. I would be here from nine in the morning till midnight and then go home and sleep and come straight back again for the next day. I couldn't sustain it, but I really loved doing it and I really loved the following year which I completely threw myself into. When we had the lantern procession coming from the city centre and we had links with four or five different organisations around Plymouth. We had a big link with the University and the Aquarium for the 'Ocean' projects.

Since doing the In the Flesh festival I got work at the Theatre Royal, I am now an associated artist there and they regularly employ me for a lot of work. Through the Barbican I started lecturing at Plymouth University and at Marjons and I get work from them quite regularly. The Barbican also support my dance theatre company, 'Symbiotic'. This organisation always feel like they are there and they are always supportive. I have been here for five-and-a-half years which is the longest I have ever lived anywhere and I have no intention of leaving.

"For the theatre to give us that space and say 'Go, on then' was great."

MARS.TARRAB

Live Performance Artists

Rachel Mars: I never considered performance as something I would do in life. But, I had an inspiring Drama Teacher so instead of doing Medieval History at Cambridge, I did English & Theatre at Leeds and came out of that with my own theatre company. I met Nat at a 'DIY' professional development course, which is run by artists for artists. ***nat.tarrab:*** I studied Drama and Technical Theatre at Uni and tried to learn everything about everything. I went on to work in stage management, technical, production, directing, design and performance. I also went to the DIY workshops, where I met young Mars.

Rachel Mars: It was jestered at DIY that there were various platform events coming up. One of them was 'In The Flesh' at The Barbican Theatre and we both applied with solo shows. Mine was called '27 Questions I Will Never Ask My Grandmother'. ***nat.tarrab:*** Mine was called 'Motherfucker'. ***Rachel Mars:*** Leading up to In The Flesh, we both got the fear about doing solo shows. We discovered a lot of commonality in our creative process and interests; a shared obsession with Dustin Hoffman, weird boy/girl stuff, queer stuff, family history Jew stuff. So we said 'Fuck it, why don't we do something together?' ***nat.tarrab:*** We came to Plymouth early, locked ourselves away for 4 days and pieced together an amalgamation of our solo shows. ***Rachel Mars:*** '27 Questions I will Never Ask My Grandmother' met 'Motherfucker' and become '27 Ways I Will Never Fuck My Mother'.

nat.tarrab: It was such a fantastic experience, completely bonkers. For the theatre to give us that space and say 'Go, on then' was great. We got a great reception, although a lot of people were somewhat overwhelmed by the insanity and absolute weirdness of it. ***Rachel Mars:*** We're now at the beginning stage of redeveloping 'Tom Boy Blues: The Theory of Dissapointment', one of 3 pieces we've made together. Through this partnership, we have Arts Council funding - and we're able to pay ourselves and we have an external directors eye in Mark Laville.

nat.tarrab: For a group who have never worked together before, there's a genuine trust. Very quickly, we have been able to get onto the same page about what we're doing, what we're saying and what we're asking with this piece of work. ***Rachel Mars:*** Tom Boy Blues is about gender identity belonging and wondering what things would be like if you weren't you. The essential questions we ask are: "Why won't I let you be you?", "Why won't I let me be me?", and "Why won't you let me be me?" They're big earnest questions to wrestle with but essentially, it's about the simplicity of being and allowing people to be who they are. ***nat.tarrab:*** Our piece, from development to execution is an experiment. I wonder whether The Barbican Theatre is unique to the South West, in terms of it's embracing and allowing new work by providing an open space for artists to experiment, go for it, and flourish in?

Rachel Mars: We fantasise continually about bringing this relationship with The Barbican Theatre forward. We hope in the future, rather than bringing a ready-made piece of work to the theatre, we can make something from nothing together. ***nat.tarrab:*** Everything we'd originally hoped for with this partnership is happening. We'd hoped for a space to develop the work, for money to pay ourselves, for an outside eye that we trust. We'd hoped for support selling the shows and for there to be money to make flyers and posters, and there is. We'd hoped to be taken seriously and we are. It's all happening here and now.

HANNAH SILVA

Spoken Word Artist,
Writer-In-Residence at Plymouth City Council

"I think emerging artists and students trying new things out have an excellent resource in the Barbican Theatre."

I first performed at the Barbican last year, with Panoctogan, for In The Flesh festival. The performance was about being seen, but not being able to see. It was like a surveillance thing but it had many different elements to it about language, belonging and identity.

I thought I'd grown out of doing scratch nights. I didn't really want to do that kind of stuff anymore. I thought In The Flesh was going to be chaotic, but it was fantastic and I was really impressed by Mark Laville. He was there in my rehearsal time, sorting out everything and running the show. I was surprised by that because usually when you take something to a theatre the artistic director won't even see it, that has been my experience before and it's really frustrating but Mark was really involved in everything.

After In the Flesh last year I kept in touch with Mark and I applied for the Flourish programme. So it was out of In the Flesh that I got the support for my new show 'Opposition'. Mark has given me some artistic input for the piece and a lot of support to make it happen, and I have some Arts Council funding which is really good.

I think emerging artists and students trying new things out have an excellent resource in the Barbican Theatre. They give a lot of support and help people move through to being professionals. It didn't happen quite that way for me because by the time I came to In the Flesh I was getting there already, having gained opportunities outside of the South West.

I think there is a clearer market for what I do in London and elsewhere, that's where people know what I am and where to place me and there's an already developed audience for the spoken word outside of the South West. However, I think Apples and Snakes have been integral in changing that here, especially with the Forked nights held at the Theatre. I also think there is room for a dialogue here that I haven't found anywhere else. At The Barbican Theatre artists are taken seriously and not patronised. I think there is an opportunity to come here with new ideas and things you want to do.

I am feeling positive about the work I am doing at the Barbican. I have also got some connections with the Theatre Royal now, and I'm Writer in Residence with the Arts Unit in Plymouth City Council so it feels like things are getting better in this area. Obviously if they stop happening and if there are opportunities elsewhere then I will have to move but I think if things keep developing and it is sustainable to be an artist down here then that is what I want to do.

"I auditioned for PYDC when I was 16 - I got in and didn't leave for another 10 years!"

AMIE LORD

Graduate Intern Laban Health

I auditioned for PYDC when I was 16 - I got in and didn't leave for another 10 years! After I left university - I was studying Contemporary Dance - the theatre gave me opportunities to train in dance leadership and choreography. I also took on shadowing roles to get more experience in choreography and to learn about where ideas for dance come from. I was able to lead sessions and eventually work freelance running dance classes at the theatre. I did some choreography with PYDC for the Cultural Olympiad and as I gained confidence I was able to go out into the community and to schools.

It has been great to see over ten years how dance performances have changed at the Barbican. When I first started, dance performances were always in the theatre. Over time, the Barbican have created more and more opportunities to take dance into the community - like the city centre and the bigger scale promenade stuff.

It's vastly improved in Plymouth from when I first started dancing. Not many schools did GCSE dance. Opportunities have now grown and the Barbican Theatre helped with that. There are now much better opportunities, Plymouth Dance, University of Plymouth…..I got lots of offers as I was leaving Plymouth and I thought 'oh no, what have I done?!'. It is fantastic to have that highly trained great dance experience on your doorstep. I know lots of people who have taken advantage of that and gone on to train at prestigious colleges in London as well other dance schools.

I moved to London in April 2010 to work as an intern with Circus Space on their intern youth programme for 3 months. Every Sunday I opened the doors to hundreds of families and young people to learn circus skills. I also helped to coordinate their summer school, a juggling parade and the end of year school for London Youth Circus. I worked at Circus Space for 3 months and ended up teaching for them. I have spent a lot of time looking for a permanent job in the art sector – it's been really difficult to find something but I've just got a job at Laban, a graduate intern position in the dance clinic. I'm the only full time member of staff and the link for everyone. I'm so happy to be getting a break really, to be doing what I love.

Dancing encompasses everything. I love being active, healthy and moving and feeling free At the same time there's the social element. When a group of people perform and make something together, you make strong friendships, really strong bonds. Through dance I've been able to experience that and there's nothing else like it, nothing else to compare it to. The experience I had at The Barbican Theatre was really integral to who and where I am now, it really influenced my life not only as a dancer but as a person. It's a special atmosphere to grow in, to build skills and confidence. It was a really fulfilling experience to be part of the place and the opportunities it gives.

SARAH PYM

Theatre Development Officer, The Works (Theatre Cornwall)

I applied for a job at the Barbican Theatre in 1995. I saw the ad in The Guardian. It was fate, really, because I'd just read an article in the Guardian about how to do your CV properly. I redid my CV, applied for the job and got it. Before, I had been working virtually unpaid at an Arts Centre which I'd helped to develop. I couldn't go on working unpaid forever, so getting the job at the theatre felt like being in the right place at the right time.

There have always been two visions to the theatre: to be a producing theatre company, producing exciting, contemporary professional work, and to be an enabling organisation for young people, creating accessible work. Sometimes these two things worked against each other, sometimes they worked very well together. Soon after I started, the building got refurbished. We had a small but working theatre which I tried to develop as a venue, where stuff was going on every week.

I think chances to see and develop experimental work are really important. Places like the Barbican Theatre are of the right scale and the right feel to actually be part of that development process.

Emerging companies need places to perform, they need a professionally run space to perform in, and they need to have the challenges and demands of working in a professional space to help them learn. To perform at the Barbican Theatre is something of a benchmark for young companies in Plymouth, I hear this from the companies themselves. It's something that they really value. You can put a piece of work up, you can debate afterwards, you can discuss and give feedback, which is useful and constructive to the company. Larger scale venues don't do that, you don't see something on the main stage of a large scale venue, then go and chat in the bar with the actors afterwards. Small theatres can do that and that's very exciting. With scratch work, you can actually feel as a member of the audience that you're giving something back, you're helping their development. How do things get better if there isn't that dialogue?

> *"If you're shown something at a fairly raw stage you feel engaged, it's more energising and you somehow want it to succeed because you feel you're on the same side."*

People like seeing work at an unpolished stage, I think it energises an audience. There's something about seeing polished work which makes you sit back and think 'entertain me, bring on the dancing girls'. If you're shown something at a fairly raw stage you feel engaged, it's more energising and you somehow want it to succeed because you feel you're on the same side. You feel that you're part of the process and I think that's really exciting; it feels like you're making theatre together rather than just observing something.

I'm very passionate about working with young people and I think the Barbican Theatre gave me that. I was a teacher, so I've always been interested in young peoples development but I think the Barbican sharpened that up for me. I was very happy there, I met wonderful people and I think it's in very good hands now. I just so wish it will survive.

CONCLUSION

This publication is a celebration of all the people who have contributed to the life of the theatre over the last 30 years. It is a symbol of collective achievement. 30 years, 30 voices comes at an uncertain time, with widespread cuts in all areas of public life. There have been difficult times in the past, and the theatre has always responded by holding a steady course guided by its values. Our bottom line is that people are the value. What we do, regardless of scale or resources, is about people working together using theatre and dance to make a difference. Together we make something that is more than the sum of its parts and together we are bigger than ourselves. We hope you will continue to help us with the journey forwards.

The Barbican Theatre has collaborated with many arts and non arts organisations. Unfortunately, we only have two pages in which to thank you all. To everyone we have worked with, a huge thank you.

Funders

Arts Council England
Plymouth City Council
Awards for All
The Baring Foundation
Creative Partnerships
Devon County Council
Devon Education Business Partnership
Enterprise Plymouth
Grass Roots Fund
Gulbenkian Foundation
Lloyds TSB Foundation
Investment Arts South West
Marks & Spencer
National Lottery Charities Board
Orange
Partnership Regeneration
Plymouth Primary and Secondary Schools
Plymouth City Council
The Princes Trust
RIO
S & W Devon Health Joint Consultative Committee
South & West Devon Health Authority
Plymouth Guild
Wellcome Trust
Young Roots Heritage Funding
Youth Opportunities Fund

Arts and Non Arts Partners

ARROW / Indra Congress
Asian Arts Agency South West
Attik Dance
Barefoot
BBC Big Screen, Plymouth
Black Police Association
Black South West Network
British Council
Brook Sexual Health Services
Christian Aid
Dance South West
Dartington College of Art & Design
Dartington Trust
Devon Road Safety Unit
Devon and Cornwall Police Constabulary Team
Devon Arts in School Initiative
Deep Blue Sound
Drakes Circus
Equality South West
Excellence Clusters
Fate.He
Ground Work Trust
KEEP
La Maison du Theatre (Brest)
Marine Biological Association
Plymouth Music Zone
Manpower Services Commission
National Children's Homes
National Marine Aquarium
National Trust (Saltram House, Mount Edgecombe, Buckland Abbey)
Nation Street Arts Festival
NSPCC
Part Exchange Co.
Pavillion Dance
Peninsula Arts
People's Institute for Survival and Beyond
Plymouth Arts Centre
Plymouth and Cornwall Primary Care Trust
Plymouth City Centre Company
Plymouth College of Art
Plymouth Culture Board
Plymouth Dance
Plymouth Jazz and Blues Festival
Plymouth Museum & Art Gallery
Plymouth Resource & Recycling
Plymouth Respect Festival
Plymouth Residents and Tennants Association
Plymouth South Asian Society
Plymouth NHS Trust
Plymouth and Devon Racial Equality Council
Plymouth Youth Offending Service
Plymouth Probation Service
Primary Care Trust
Rambert Dance Company
Refugee Action
Refugee First
Schools Linking Network
Stiltskin Theatre Company
Streets of the South West Partners
Sure Start
Theatre Royal & TR2
The Works (Theatre and Dance Cornwall)
The Prison Service
University College Marjons
University of Plymouth
Urban Splash
Zap Productions

theatre
b
café
bar

THANKS

Thanks to all involved in the production of this book

Author
Pamela Peter-Agbia

Editor / Contributor
Kate Campbell

Design
William Hibberd

Photography
Jay Bing
Oliver Alexander-Jones
Josh Greet
Dom Moore
Viktoria Begg
Patrick Chinery

Archive Photography
Kevin Clifford
Gemma Ward
Wayne Perry

Video
Lauri Fowler

Publishing
Paul Honeywill

Special thanks to
Catharine Chapman
Luke Broadway
Matthew Pontin
Jonathan Blythe
Drew Turner
Matrix Design
Plymouth College of Art
University of Plymouth

itc Approved Manager Member

Supported by ARTS COUNCIL ENGLAND

PLYMOUTH CITY COUNCIL